Solve each problem. Use the ke

8 = green   9 = blue   10 = red   II

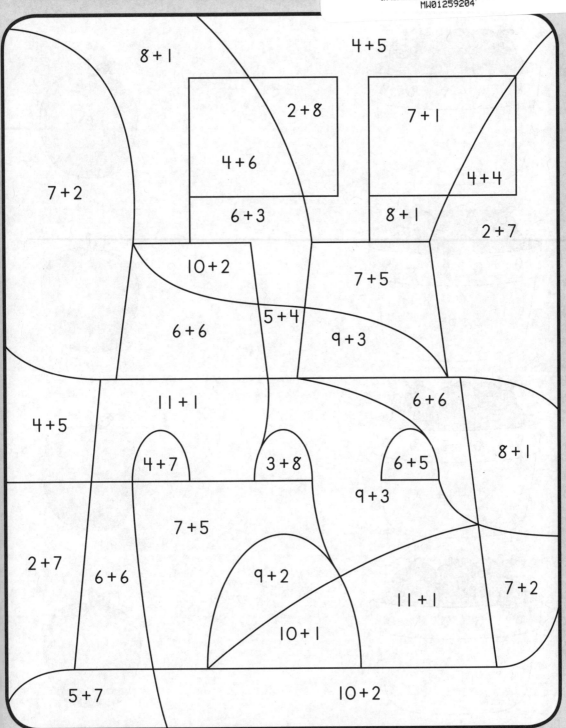

Solve each problem. Draw a line to match each problem to the correct sum.

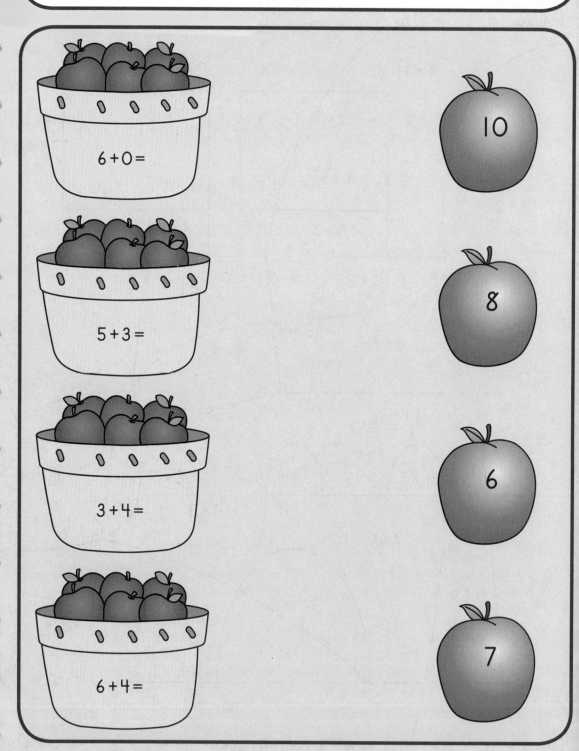

6 + 0 =

10

5 + 3 =

8

3 + 4 =

6

6 + 4 =

7

CD-104366

Solve each word problem.

1. Scott picked 7 baskets of berries. Dawson picked 5 baskets of berries. How many baskets of berries did the boys pick altogether?

2. Kayla planted 4 flowers. Claire planted 7 flowers. How many flowers did the girls plant altogether?

3. Jeremy planted 6 rosebushes. Gabe planted 6 rosebushes. How many rosebushes did the boys plant altogether?

4. Keisha and Myla went to the library. Each girl checked out 3 books about flowers. How many books did the girls check out altogether?

Solve each problem.

$$\begin{array}{r} 1 \\ 2 \\ +\ 4 \\ \hline \end{array}$$

$$\begin{array}{r} 3 \\ 1 \\ +\ 4 \\ \hline \end{array}$$

$$\begin{array}{r} 2 \\ 2 \\ +\ 4 \\ \hline \end{array}$$

$$\begin{array}{r} 1 \\ 4 \\ +\ 4 \\ \hline \end{array}$$

$$\begin{array}{r} 1 \\ 5 \\ +\ 4 \\ \hline \end{array}$$

$$\begin{array}{r} 1 \\ 2 \\ +\ 0 \\ \hline \end{array}$$

$$\begin{array}{r} 3 \\ 4 \\ +\ 3 \\ \hline \end{array}$$

$$\begin{array}{r} 2 \\ 2 \\ +\ 1 \\ \hline \end{array}$$

$$\begin{array}{r} 6 \\ 1 \\ +\ 3 \\ \hline \end{array}$$

$$\begin{array}{r} 6 \\ 2 \\ +\ 2 \\ \hline \end{array}$$

$$\begin{array}{r} 5 \\ 2 \\ +\ 1 \\ \hline \end{array}$$

$$\begin{array}{r} 8 \\ 1 \\ +\ 1 \\ \hline \end{array}$$

CD-104366

Solve each word problem.

1. Riley has 3 striped cats, 2 gray cats, and 1 white cat. How many cats does Riley have altogether?

2. Oliver saw 2 green hummingbirds, 1 blue hummingbird, and 1 red hummingbird. How many hummingbirds did Oliver see altogether?

3. Raul has 3 yellow fish, 5 red fish, and 2 green fish. How many fish does Raul have altogether?

4. It snowed 2 days in December, 4 days in January, and 3 days in February. How many days did it snow altogether?

Solve each problem. Use the key to color the picture.
8 = orange   9 = green   10 = red   11 = yellow

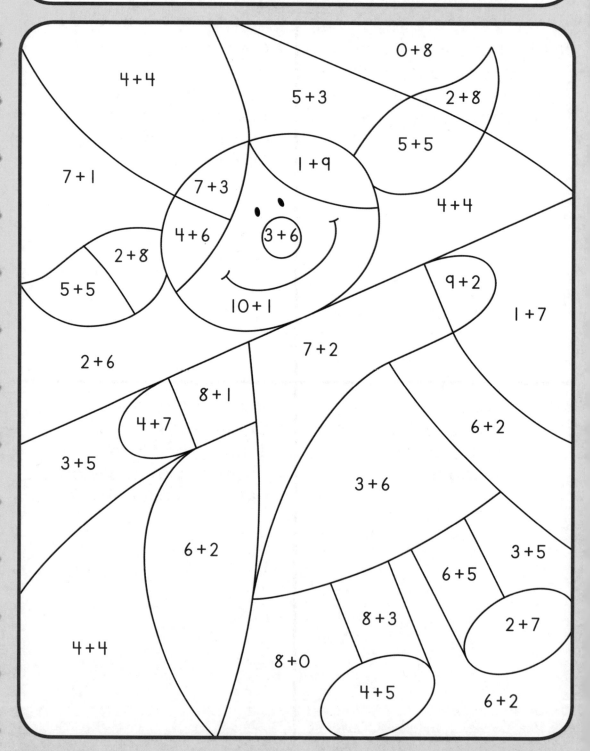

CD-104366

Solve each problem.

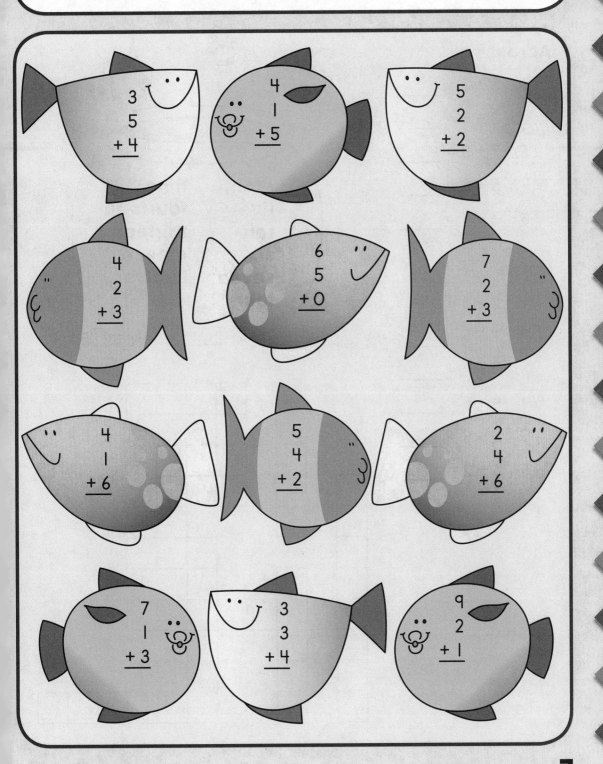

$$\begin{array}{r} 3 \\ 5 \\ +\ 4 \\ \hline \end{array}$$

$$\begin{array}{r} 4 \\ 1 \\ +\ 5 \\ \hline \end{array}$$

$$\begin{array}{r} 5 \\ 2 \\ +\ 2 \\ \hline \end{array}$$

$$\begin{array}{r} 4 \\ 2 \\ +\ 3 \\ \hline \end{array}$$

$$\begin{array}{r} 6 \\ 5 \\ +\ 0 \\ \hline \end{array}$$

$$\begin{array}{r} 7 \\ 2 \\ +\ 3 \\ \hline \end{array}$$

$$\begin{array}{r} 4 \\ 1 \\ +\ 6 \\ \hline \end{array}$$

$$\begin{array}{r} 5 \\ 4 \\ +\ 2 \\ \hline \end{array}$$

$$\begin{array}{r} 2 \\ 4 \\ +\ 6 \\ \hline \end{array}$$

$$\begin{array}{r} 7 \\ 1 \\ +\ 3 \\ \hline \end{array}$$

$$\begin{array}{r} 3 \\ 3 \\ +\ 4 \\ \hline \end{array}$$

$$\begin{array}{r} 9 \\ 2 \\ +\ 1 \\ \hline \end{array}$$

Solve each problem. Write the number words to complete the crossword puzzle.

Across

1. 3 + 1 = ____
2. 3 + 4 = ____
5. 7 + 3 = ____
7. 5 + 8 = ____
8. 7 + 4 = ____

Down

1. 2 + 3 = ____
2. 1 + 5 = ____
3. 5 + 4 = ____
4. 9 + 5 = ____
5. 8 + 4 = ____
6. 6 + 2 = ____

eight   nine
five   fourteen
ten   thirteen
six   eleven
seven   twelve
four

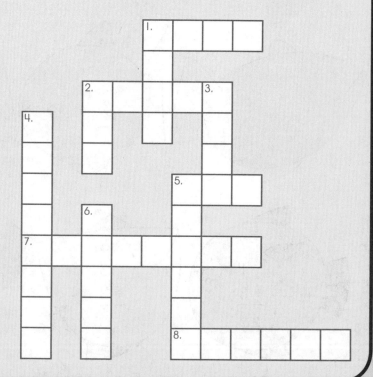

CD-104366

Solve each problem. Circle the problems in each row with sums equal to the number on the birdhouse.

6 2 + 5	5 5 + 8	7 4 + 7

9 2 + 5	7 5 + 1	8 6 + 2

6 4 + 5	5 5 + 5	7 4 + 3

6 1 + 5	5 3 + 2	6 3 + 3

Solve each problem. Draw a line to match each problem to the correct sum.

$7 + 7 =$ 5

$6 + 4 =$ 6

$2 + 3 =$ 7

$13 + 3 =$ 8

$0 + 9 =$ 9

$3 + 4 =$ 10

$12 + 3 =$ 11

$4 + 2 =$ 12

$10 + 2 =$ 13

$4 + 7 =$ 14

$6 + 7 =$ 15

$5 + 3 =$ 16

CD-104366

Solve each word problem.

1. Nadia and her father grew pumpkins in their garden. They gave 7 away, they entered 2 in the fair, and they made pies with 5 pumpkins. How many total pumpkins did they grow?

2. Taylor collected items during a hike. He collected 8 rocks, 3 pinecones, and 6 flowers. How many total items did Taylor collect?

3. Andrew and his mother picked 4 bushels of apples on Thursday, 7 bushels on Friday, and 7 bushels on Saturday. How many total bushels of apples did they pick?

4. Ian walks his neighbors' dogs during the summer. He walks 7 poodles, 3 collies, and 6 beagles. How many dogs does he walk altogether?

Solve each problem. Follow the problems that equal 18 to help the pilot find the airplane.

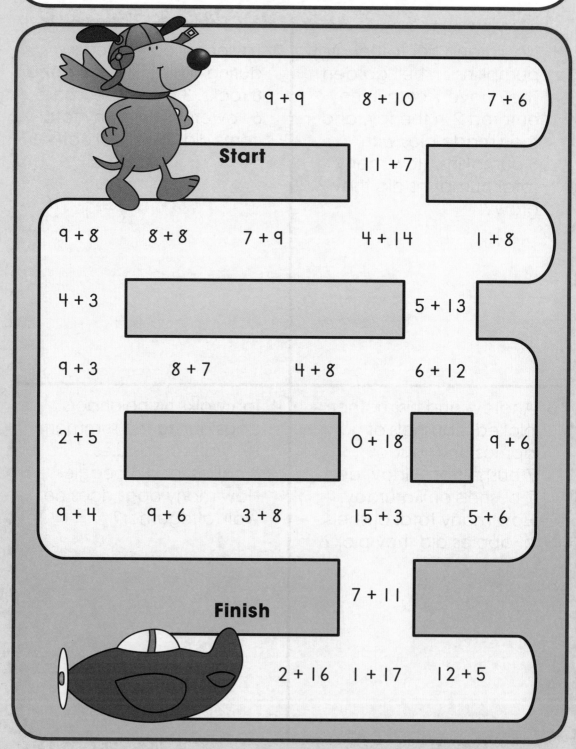

9 + 9   8 + 10   7 + 6

Start   11 + 7

9 + 8   8 + 8   7 + 9   4 + 14   1 + 8

4 + 3   5 + 13

9 + 3   8 + 7   4 + 8   6 + 12

2 + 5   0 + 18   9 + 6

9 + 4   9 + 6   3 + 8   15 + 3   5 + 6

Finish   7 + 11

2 + 16   1 + 17   12 + 5

CD-104366

Write the missing numbers to solve each problem. The first one has been done for you.

Problem 1:
$$2 + 7 = 9$$
$$+ \quad +$$
$$7 + 4 = 11$$
$$\overline{9} \quad \overline{11}$$

Problem 2:
$$\square + \square = 11$$
$$+ \quad +$$
$$\square + \square = 12$$
$$\overline{11} \quad \overline{12}$$

Problem 3:
$$\square + \square = 8$$
$$+ \quad +$$
$$\square + \square = 3$$
$$+ \quad +$$
$$\square + \square = 15$$
$$\overline{11} \quad \overline{15}$$

Problem 4:
$$\square + \square = 10$$
$$+ \quad +$$
$$\square + \square = 7$$
$$+ \quad +$$
$$\square + \square = 16$$
$$\overline{15} \quad \overline{18}$$

Solve each problem. Draw a line to match each problem to the correct sum.

7
3
+ 6

17

4
9
+ 5

16

2
7
+ 3

18

4
8
+ 5

12

CD-104366

Write the missing numbers from each fact family to complete the number sentences.

4, 6, 10

☐ + 4 = 10

4 + 6 = ☐

10 − ☐ = 6

☐ − 6 = 4

3, 6, 9

☐ + 3 = 9

3 + 6 = ☐

9 − ☐ = 6

☐ − 6 = 3

2, 5, 7

☐ + 5 = 7

5 + 2 = ☐

7 − ☐ = 2

☐ − 2 = 5

3, 7, 10

☐ + 3 = 10

3 + 7 = ☐

10 − ☐ = 7

☐ − 7 = 3

CD-104366

Solve each problem.

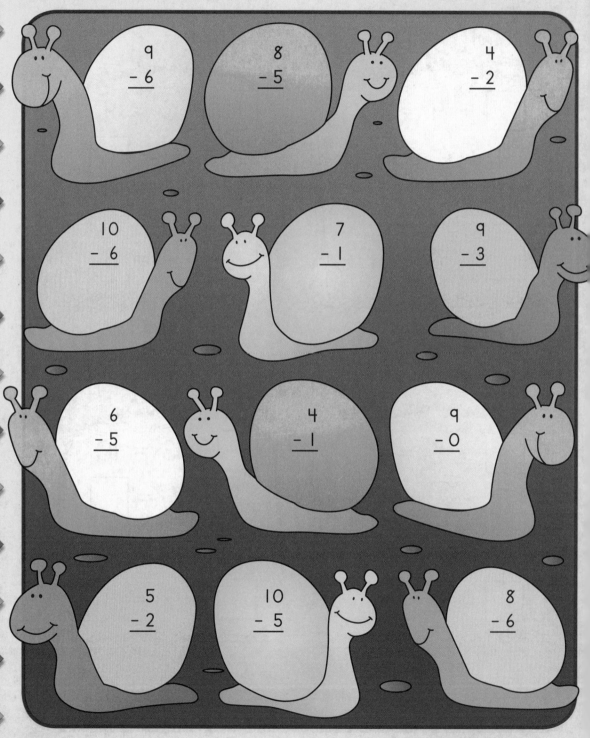

$$\begin{array}{r} 9 \\ -6 \\ \hline \end{array}$$

$$\begin{array}{r} 8 \\ -5 \\ \hline \end{array}$$

$$\begin{array}{r} 4 \\ -2 \\ \hline \end{array}$$

$$\begin{array}{r} 10 \\ -6 \\ \hline \end{array}$$

$$\begin{array}{r} 7 \\ -1 \\ \hline \end{array}$$

$$\begin{array}{r} 9 \\ -3 \\ \hline \end{array}$$

$$\begin{array}{r} 6 \\ -5 \\ \hline \end{array}$$

$$\begin{array}{r} 4 \\ -1 \\ \hline \end{array}$$

$$\begin{array}{r} 9 \\ -0 \\ \hline \end{array}$$

$$\begin{array}{r} 5 \\ -2 \\ \hline \end{array}$$

$$\begin{array}{r} 10 \\ -5 \\ \hline \end{array}$$

$$\begin{array}{r} 8 \\ -6 \\ \hline \end{array}$$

 CD-104366

Solve each problem. Use the key to color the picture.
7 = yellow   8 = red   9 = blue   10 = black

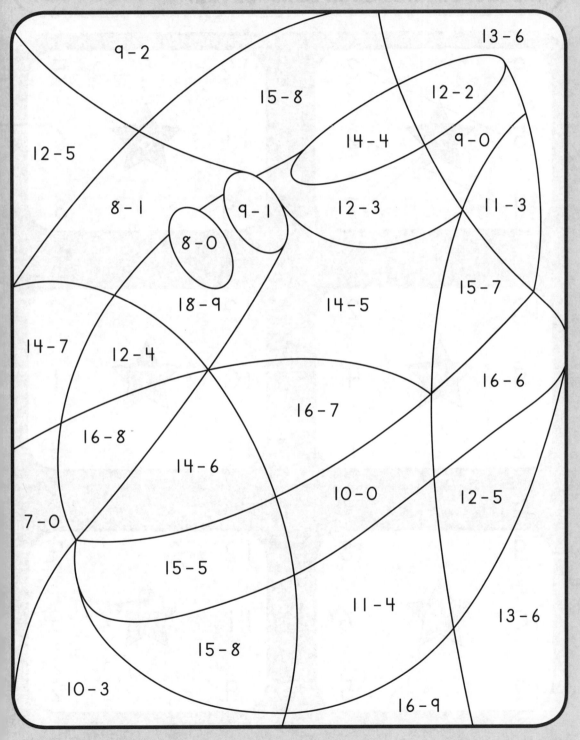

9 – 2

13 – 6

15 – 8

12 – 2

14 – 4

9 – 0

12 – 5

8 – 1

9 – 1

12 – 3

11 – 3

8 – 0

18 – 9

14 – 5

15 – 7

14 – 7

12 – 4

16 – 6

16 – 7

16 – 8

14 – 6

10 – 0

12 – 5

7 – 0

15 – 5

11 – 4

13 – 6

15 – 8

10 – 3

16 – 9

CD-104366

17

Draw a line to connect each pair of numbers whose difference equals the number in the star. The first one has been done for you.

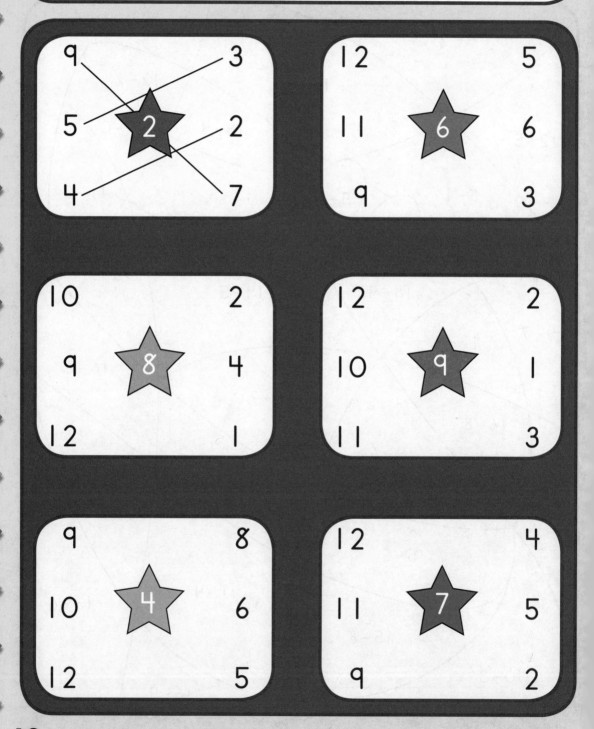

CD-104366 © Carson-Dellosa

Write the missing numbers from each fact family to complete the number sentences.

2, 3, 5

☐ + 3 = 5

3 + 2 = ☐

5 − ☐ = 2

☐ − 2 = 3

4, 5, 9

☐ + 4 = 9

4 + 5 = ☐

9 − ☐ = 5

☐ − 5 = 4

2, 4, 6

☐ + 4 = 6

4 + 2 = ☐

6 − ☐ = 2

☐ − 2 = 4

2, 8, 10

☐ + 2 = 10

2 + 8 = ☐

10 − ☐ = 8

☐ − 8 = 2

Solve each word problem.

1. Aaron saw 10 cardinals and 7 blue jays. How many more cardinals than blue jays did Aaron see?

2. Michelle counted 9 squirrels in her yard. Four of the squirrels ran to another yard. How many squirrels are left in Michelle's yard?

3. Gavin has 8 bird feeders to fill. He has filled 3 bird feeders. How many more bird feeders does Gavin have to fill?

4. Amelia saw 10 butterflies in the garden. Six of the butterflies flew away. How many butterflies are left in the garden?

CD-104366

Solve each problem.

$$\begin{array}{r} 16 \\ -\ 6 \\ \hline \end{array}$$

$$\begin{array}{r} 14 \\ -12 \\ \hline \end{array}$$

$$\begin{array}{r} 12 \\ -\ 7 \\ \hline \end{array}$$

$$\begin{array}{r} 13 \\ -10 \\ \hline \end{array}$$

$$\begin{array}{r} 9 \\ -1 \\ \hline \end{array}$$

$$\begin{array}{r} 8 \\ -\ 4 \\ \hline \end{array}$$

$$\begin{array}{r} 10 \\ -\ 0 \\ \hline \end{array}$$

$$\begin{array}{r} 16 \\ -\ 1 \\ \hline \end{array}$$

$$\begin{array}{r} 15 \\ -11 \\ \hline \end{array}$$

$$\begin{array}{r} 12 \\ -\ 5 \\ \hline \end{array}$$

$$\begin{array}{r} 15 \\ -\ 5 \\ \hline \end{array}$$

$$\begin{array}{r} 11 \\ -\ 8 \\ \hline \end{array}$$

CD-104366

Solve each problem. Use the key to color the picture.
8 = blue 9 = brown 10 = red 11 = green 12 = yellow

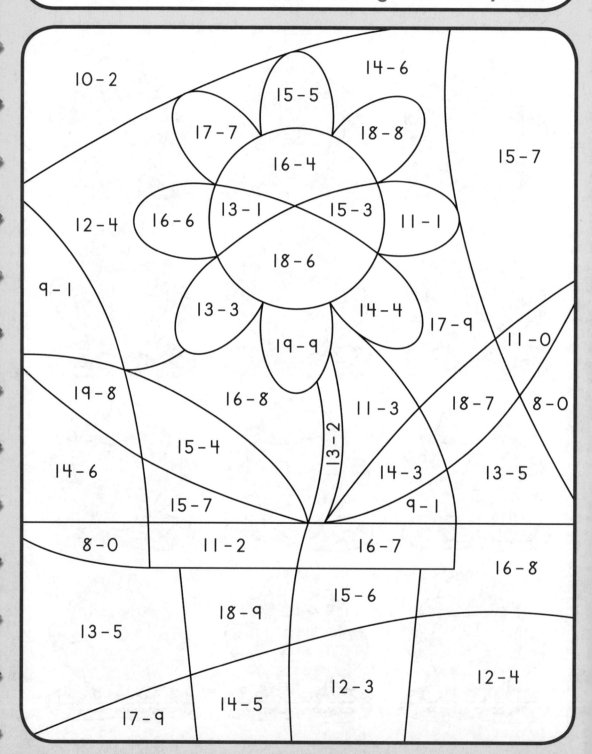

10 - 2

14 - 6

15 - 5

17 - 7

18 - 8

16 - 4

15 - 7

16 - 6

13 - 1

15 - 3

11 - 1

12 - 4

18 - 6

9 - 1

13 - 3

14 - 4

17 - 9

19 - 9

11 - 0

19 - 8

16 - 8

11 - 3

18 - 7

8 - 0

13 - 2

15 - 4

14 - 6

14 - 3

13 - 5

15 - 7

9 - 1

8 - 0

11 - 2

16 - 7

16 - 8

15 - 6

18 - 9

13 - 5

12 - 4

12 - 3

14 - 5

17 - 9

CD-104366

© Carson-Dellosa

Solve each problem.

$$17 - 13$$

$$19 - 11$$

$$18 - 3$$

$$13 - 8$$

$$19 - 12$$

$$17 - 6$$

$$8 - 2$$

$$18 - 8$$

$$15 - 7$$

$$16 - 9$$

$$14 - 2$$

$$10 - 8$$

CD-104366

Solve each problem. Write the number words to complete the crossword puzzle.

fifteen   fourteen
eleven   eighteen
ten   seventeen
sixteen   thirteen
nine   twelve

Across
2. 15 – 3 = ___
3. 13 – 4 = ___
5. 16 – 3 = ___
7. 18 – 3 = ___
8. 18 – 0 = ___
9. 18 – 1 = ___

Down
1. 16 – 2 = ___
2. 17 – 7 = ___
4. 15 – 4 = ___
6. 18 – 2 = ___

CD-104366

Solve each problem. Draw a line to match each problem to the correct difference.

14 – 5 =	18
17 – 3 =	17
18 – 3 =	16
16 – 3 =	15
15 – 7 =	14
18 – 1 =	13
16 – 9 =	12
17 – 7 =	11
14 – 2 =	10
17 – 1 =	9
18 – 0 =	8
15 – 4 =	7

Write the missing numbers from each fact family to complete the number sentences.

7, 8, 15

$\boxed{} + 8 = 15$

$8 + 7 = \boxed{}$

$15 - \boxed{} = 7$

$\boxed{} - 7 = 8$

6, 9, 15

$\boxed{} + 6 = 15$

$6 + 9 = \boxed{}$

$15 - \boxed{} = 9$

$\boxed{} - 9 = 6$

5, 7, 12

$\boxed{} + 5 = 12$

$5 + 7 = \boxed{}$

$12 - \boxed{} = 7$

$\boxed{} - 7 = 5$

2, 10, 12

$\boxed{} + 2 = 12$

$2 + 10 = \boxed{}$

$12 - \boxed{} = 10$

$\boxed{} - 10 = 2$

CD-104366

Solve each problem. Match the sums to the numbers below. Write the correct letters on the lines.

What is a rabbit's favorite game?

$10 - 1 =$ _____ (O) $5 + 5 =$ _____ (H)

$10 - 3 =$ _____ (S) $10 - 5 =$ _____ (T)

$5 + 3 =$ _____ (P) $2 + 4 =$ _____ (C)

| 10 | 9 | 8 | 7 | 6 | 9 | 5 | 6 | 10 |

CD-104366

Solve each problem. Use the key to color the melons.
Equal to 6 = orange   Greater than 6 = yellow
Less than 6 = green

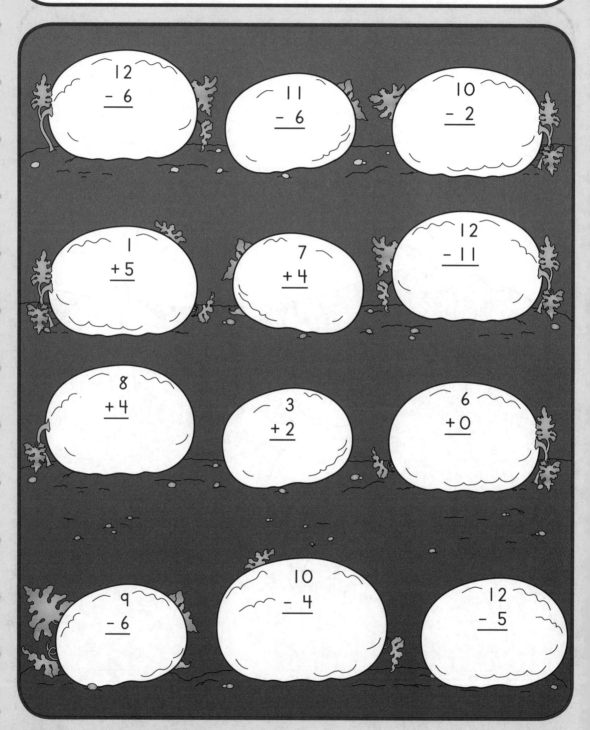

$$\begin{array}{r} 12 \\ -\ 6 \\ \hline \end{array}$$

$$\begin{array}{r} 11 \\ -\ 6 \\ \hline \end{array}$$

$$\begin{array}{r} 10 \\ -\ 2 \\ \hline \end{array}$$

$$\begin{array}{r} 1 \\ +5 \\ \hline \end{array}$$

$$\begin{array}{r} 7 \\ +4 \\ \hline \end{array}$$

$$\begin{array}{r} 12 \\ -11 \\ \hline \end{array}$$

$$\begin{array}{r} 8 \\ +4 \\ \hline \end{array}$$

$$\begin{array}{r} 3 \\ +2 \\ \hline \end{array}$$

$$\begin{array}{r} 6 \\ +0 \\ \hline \end{array}$$

$$\begin{array}{r} 9 \\ -6 \\ \hline \end{array}$$

$$\begin{array}{r} 10 \\ -\ 4 \\ \hline \end{array}$$

$$\begin{array}{r} 12 \\ -\ 5 \\ \hline \end{array}$$

28 CD-104366

Write the missing numbers from each fact family to complete the number sentences.

4, 10, 14

$\boxed{} + 4 = 14$

$4 + 10 = \boxed{}$

$14 - \boxed{} = 10$

$\boxed{} - 10 = 4$

6, 8, 14

$\boxed{} + 6 = 14$

$6 + 8 = \boxed{}$

$14 - \boxed{} = 8$

$\boxed{} - 8 = 6$

6, 7, 13

$\boxed{} + 6 = 13$

$6 + 7 = \boxed{}$

$13 - \boxed{} = 7$

$\boxed{} - 7 = 6$

5, 8, 13

$\boxed{} + 5 = 13$

$5 + 8 = \boxed{}$

$13 - \boxed{} = 8$

$\boxed{} - 8 = 5$

CD-104366

29

Solve each problem. Use the key to color the picture.
9 = blue   10 = pink   11 = yellow   12 = brown

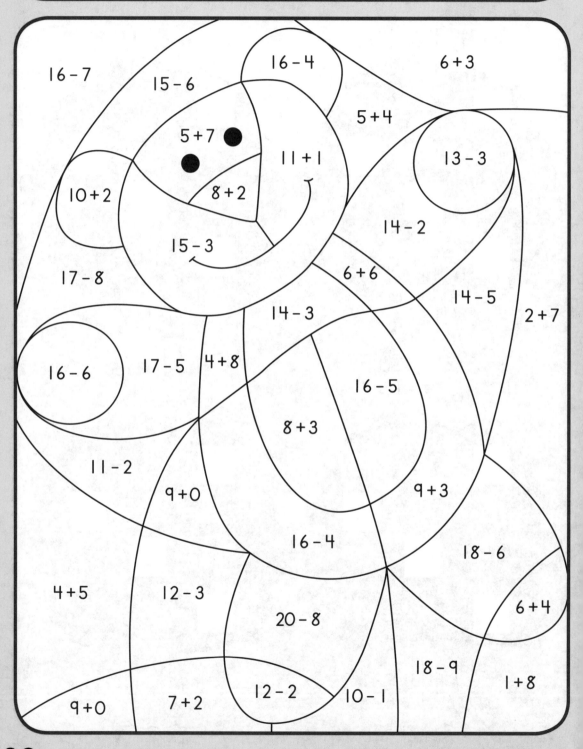

16 − 7

15 − 6

16 − 4

6 + 3

5 + 4

5 + 7

11 + 1

13 − 3

10 + 2

8 + 2

15 − 3

14 − 2

17 − 8

6 + 6

14 − 5

14 − 3

2 + 7

16 − 6

17 − 5

4 + 8

16 − 5

8 + 3

11 − 2

9 + 0

9 + 3

16 − 4

18 − 6

4 + 5

12 − 3

6 + 4

20 − 8

18 − 9

1 + 8

9 + 0

7 + 2

12 − 2

10 − 1

CD-104366

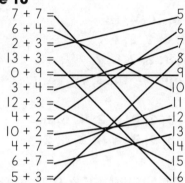

Page 1
The picture should show a sand castle.

Page 2

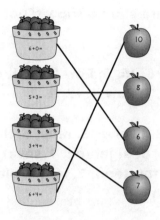

Page 3
1. 12 baskets of berries; 2. 11 flowers; 3. 12 rosebushes; 4. 6 books

Page 4
Row 1: 7, 8, 8; Row 2: 9, 10, 3; Row 3: 10, 5, 10; Row 4: 10, 8, 10

Page 5
1. 6 cats; 2. 4 hummingbirds; 3. 10 fish; 4. 9 days

Page 6
The picture should show a doll.

Page 7
Row 1: 12, 10, 9; Row 2: 9, 11, 12; Row 3: 11, 11, 12; Row 4: 11, 10, 12

Page 8
Across: 1. four; 2. seven; 5. ten; 7. thirteen; 8. eleven; Down: 1. five; 2. six; 3. nine; 4. fourteen; 5. twelve; 6. eight

Page 9
Row 1: 13, 18, 18; 5 + 5 + 8 and 7 + 4 + 7 should be circled; Row 2: 16, 13, 16; 9 + 2 + 5 and 8 + 6 + 2 should be circled; Row 3: 15, 15, 14; 6 + 4 + 5 and 5 + 5 + 5 should be circled; Row 4: 12, 10, 12; 6 + 1 + 5 and 6 + 3 + 3 should be circled.

Page 10
$7 + 7 =$
$6 + 4 =$
$2 + 3 =$
$13 + 3 =$
$0 + 9 =$
$3 + 4 =$
$12 + 3 =$
$4 + 2 =$
$10 + 2 =$
$4 + 7 =$
$6 + 7 =$
$5 + 3 =$

5
6
7
8
9
10
11
12
13
14
15
16

Page 11
1. 14 pumpkins; 2. 17 items; 3. 18 bushels of apples; 4. 16 dogs

Page 12
These problems should be followed:
9 + 9, 8 + 10, 11 + 7, 4 + 14, 5 + 13, 6 + 12, 0 + 18, 15 + 3, 7 + 11, 1 + 17, 2 + 16.

Page 13
Answers will vary but may include:
Top right: (across) 6 + 5, 5 + 7; (down) 6 + 5, 5 + 7;
Bottom left: (across) 3 + 5, 2 + 1, 6 + 9; (down) 3 + 2 + 6 and 5 + 1 + 9;
Bottom right: (across) 4 + 6, 3 + 4, 8 + 8; (down) 4 + 3 + 8, 6 + 4 + 8

Page 14

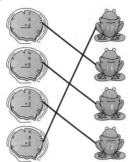

Page 15

Top left: 6, 10, 4, 10
Top right: 6, 9, 3, 9
Bottom left: 2, 7, 5, 7
Bottom right: 7, 10, 3, 10

Page 16

Row 1: 3, 3, 2; Row 2: 4, 6, 6;
Row 3: 1, 3, 9; Row 4: 3, 5, 2

Page 17

The picture should show a sneaker.

Page 18

Page 19

Top left: 2, 5, 3, 5
Top right: 5, 9, 4, 9
Bottom left: 2, 6, 4, 6
Bottom right: 8, 10, 2, 10

Page 20

1. 3 cardinals; 2. 5 squirrels;
3. 5 bird feeders; 4. 4 butterflies

Page 21

Row 1: 10, 2, 5; Row 2: 3, 8, 4;
Row 3: 10, 15, 4; Row 4: 7, 10, 3

Page 22

The picture should show a potted flower.

Page 23

Row 1: 4, 8, 15, 5; Row 2: 7, 11, 6, 10;
Row 3: 8, 7; Row 4: 12, 2

Page 24

Across: 2. twelve; 3. nine; 5. thirteen;
7. fifteen; 8. eighteen; 9. seventeen;
Down: 1. fourteen; 2. ten; 4. eleven;
6. sixteen

Page 25

```
14 – 5 =                    18
17 – 3 =                    17
18 – 3 =                    16
16 – 3 =                    15
15 – 7 =                    14
18 – 1 =                    13
16 – 9 =                    12
17 – 7 =                    11
14 – 2 =                    10
17 – 1 =                     9
18 – 0 =                     8
15 – 4 =                     7
```

Page 26

Top left: 7, 15, 8, 15
Top right: 9, 15, 6, 15
Bottom left: 7, 12, 5, 12
Bottom right: 10, 12, 2, 12

Page 27

Row 1: 9, 10; Row 2: 7, 5;
Row 3: 8, 6; Hopscotch

Page 28

Row 1: 6, 5, 8 (orange, green, yellow)
Row 2: 6, 11, 1 (orange, yellow, green)
Row 3: 12, 5, 6 (yellow, green, orange)
Row 4: 3, 6, 7 (green, orange, yellow)

Page 29
Top left: 10, 14, 4, 14
Top right: 8, 14, 6, 14
Bottom left: 7, 13, 6, 13
Bottom right: 8, 13, 5, 13
Page 30
The picture should show a teddy bear.
Page 31
Top left: 9, 16, 7, 16
Top right: 11, 16, 5, 16
Bottom left: 10, 15, 5, 15
Bottom right: 11, 15, 4, 15
Page 32
From bee to hive: 8, 16, 8, 12, 12, 15, 7, 13, 8, 6, 11, 15, 15, 10, 7, 16
Page 33
The picture should show an umbrella.
Page 34
Across: 1. fourteen; 4. nine; 5. twelve; 6. sixteen; 7. eleven; 8. ten; 9. eighteen; Down: 2. thirteen; 3. fifteen; 6. seventeen
Page 35
Top left: 11, 18, 7, 18
Top right: 9, 17, 8, 17
Bottom left: 11, 16, 5, 16
Bottom right: 9, 13, 4, 13
Page 36

13 – 6 =	7
12 + 3 =	8
12 – 4 =	9
16 + 2 =	10
15 – 5 =	11
18 – 6 =	12
11 + 6 =	13
17 – 3 =	14
14 – 5 =	15
9 + 7 =	16
18 – 7 =	17
15 – 2 =	18

Page 37
Row 1: 19, 67, 78, 28, 35, 29;
Row 2: 59, 38, 49, 68, 97; Add fourteen "carrots"!
Page 38
From top to bottom:
Column 1: 14, 21, 30, 38, 41
Column 2: 41, 44, 49, 51, 60, 67
Column 3: 67, 76, 83, 92, 93, 99
Page 39

Page 41
Row 1: 9, 25, 32, 8, 49, 79
Row 2: 48, 76, 45, 19, 69, 47
Row 3: 46, 58, 79, 20, 35, 18
The maze should follow the numbers 9, 25, 32, 8, 49, 79, 48, 76, 45, 19, 69, 47, 46, 58, 79, 20, 35, 18.
Page 42
Row 1: 23, 50, 61, 33, 60, 84;
Row 2: 58, 85, 39, 70, 57, 44;
Row 3: 63, 40, 31, 86; "Hare" spray
Page 43
The picture should show an owl.
Page 44
The picture should show a lighthouse.
Page 45

C

Page 47
Row 1: 3, 43, 21, 55, 78, 71
Row 2: 11, 73, 28, 24, 41, 61
The maze should follow the numbers 3, 43, 21, 55, 78, 71, 11, 73, 28, 24, 41, 61.

Page 48
Row 1: 307, 559, 449, 145, 427
Row 2: 824, 347, 219, 603
It had a better bark!

Page 49
Row 1: 493, 654, 801, 421, 861
Row 2: 778, 520, 212, 594, 321
Put it on my bill!

Page 50
Row 1: 348, 435, 593, 285
Row 2: 199, 277, 588, 459
Row 3: 299, 693, 799, 987
Row 4: 579, 349, 434, 267

Page 51
Row 1: 599, 587, 948, 168
Row 2: 435, 869, 147, 395
Row 3: 849, 745, 289, 894
Row 4: 579, 956, 493, 280

Page 52
Row 1: 953, 507, 840
Row 2: 217, 438, 411, 910
Row 3: 210, 521, 811, 230
Row 4: 519, 510, 802

Page 53
Row 1: 132
Row 2: 237, 421, 111
Row 3: 200, 350, 432, 804
Row 4: 201, 311, 753, 820
Row 5: 611, 254

Page 54
Row 1: 747, 985, 949, 267
Row 2: 779, 499, 697, 559
Row 3: 409, 489, 340, 979
Row 4: 255, 879, 399, 501

Page 55
1. 210 pennies; 2. 352 pieces of litter; 3. 222 items; 4. 579 items

Page 56
Row 1: 221, 22, 101, 110
Row 2: 110, 316, 476, 416
Row 3: 23, 185, 614, 311
Row 4: 112, 2, 131, 100

Page 57
1. 437 flowers; 2. 100 large jars; 3. 27 seashells; 4. 211 books

Page 58
From left to right and top to bottom:
A. 33, 77, 199, 102, 33, 69, 509, 130, 33; B. 1, 1, 1, 58, 101, 155, 346, 61, 69; C. 190, 0, 50, 110, 50, 38, 50, 10, 148; D. 85, 6, 20, 76, 20, 110, 20, 471, 88

Page 59

Write the missing numbers from each fact family to complete the number sentences.

7, 9, 16

$\boxed{} + 7 = 16$

$7 + 9 = \boxed{}$

$16 - \boxed{} = 9$

$\boxed{} - 9 = 7$

5, 11, 16

$\boxed{} + 5 = 16$

$5 + 11 = \boxed{}$

$16 - \boxed{} = 11$

$\boxed{} - 11 = 5$

5, 10, 15

$\boxed{} + 5 = 15$

$5 + 10 = \boxed{}$

$15 - \boxed{} = 10$

$\boxed{} - 10 = 5$

4, 11, 15

$\boxed{} + 4 = 15$

$4 + 11 = \boxed{}$

$15 - \boxed{} = 11$

$\boxed{} - 11 = 4$

Solve each problem to help the bee find the hive.

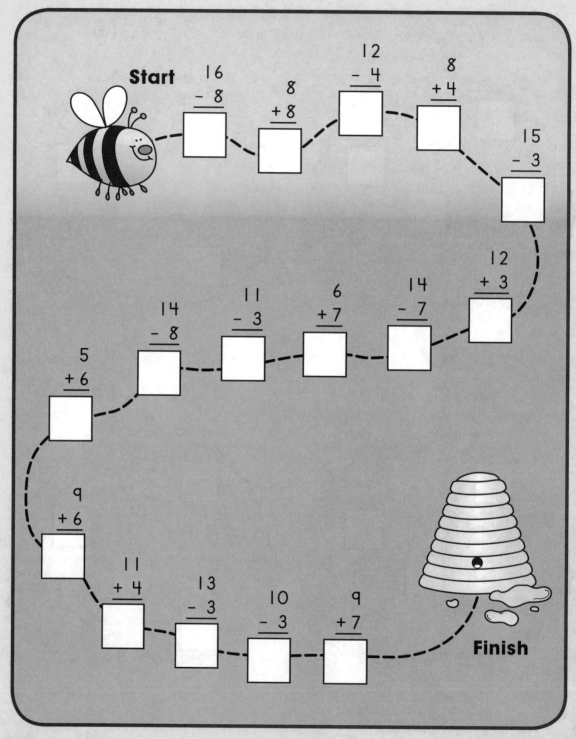

Start

16
− 8

8
+ 8

12
− 4

8
+ 4

15
− 3

12
+ 3

14
− 7

6
+ 7

11
− 3

14
− 8

5
+ 6

9
+ 6

11
+ 4

13
− 3

10
− 3

9
+ 7

Finish

Solve each problem. Use the key to color the picture.
11 = blue   12 = orange   13 = yellow   14 = red

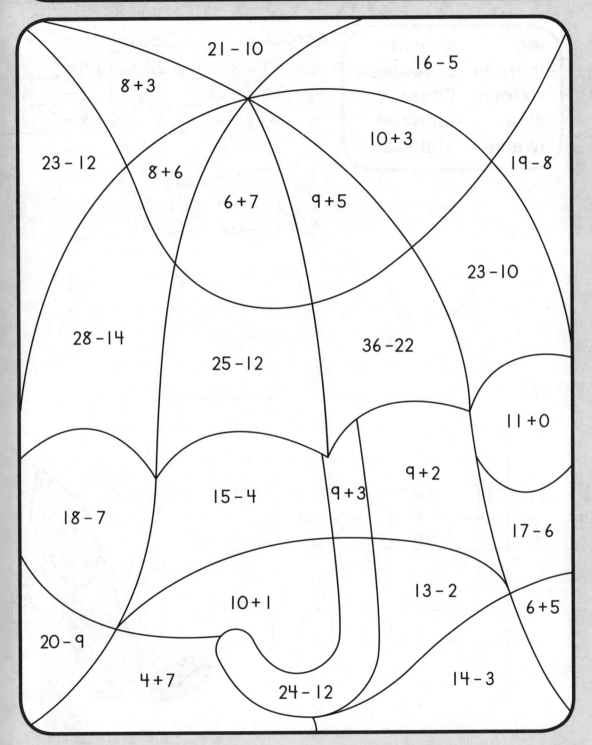

21 – 10

16 – 5

8 + 3

10 + 3

23 – 12

8 + 6

19 – 8

6 + 7

9 + 5

23 – 10

28 – 14

25 – 12

36 – 22

11 + 0

9 + 2

15 – 4

9 + 3

18 – 7

17 – 6

13 – 2

10 + 1

6 + 5

20 – 9

4 + 7

14 – 3

24 – 12

Solve each problem. Write the number words to complete the crossword puzzle.

ten	eleven
thirteen	seventeen
sixteen	fifteen
nine	fourteen
twelve	eighteen

Across

1. $17 - 3 =$ ___
4. $13 - 4 =$ ___
5. $10 + 2 =$ ___
6. $18 - 2 =$ ___
7. $17 - 6 =$ ___
8. $15 - 5 =$ ___
9. $18 - 0 =$ ___

Down

2. $9 + 4 =$ ___
3. $14 + 1 =$ ___
6. $9 + 8 =$ ___

CD-104366

Write the missing numbers from each fact family to complete the number sentences.

7, 11, 18

$\boxed{} + 7 = 18$

$7 + 11 = \boxed{}$

$18 - \boxed{} = 11$

$\boxed{} - 11 = 7$

8, 9, 17

$\boxed{} + 8 = 17$

$8 + 9 = \boxed{}$

$17 - \boxed{} = 9$

$\boxed{} - 9 = 8$

5, 11, 16

$\boxed{} + 5 = 16$

$5 + 11 = \boxed{}$

$16 - \boxed{} = 11$

$\boxed{} - 11 = 5$

4, 9, 13

$\boxed{} + 4 = 13$

$4 + 9 = \boxed{}$

$13 - \boxed{} = 9$

$\boxed{} - 9 = 4$

CD-104366

35

13 – 6 =   7

12 + 3 =   8

12 – 4 =   9

16 + 2 =   10

15 – 5 =   11

18 – 6 =   12

11 + 6 =   13

17 – 3 =   14

14 – 5 =   15

9 + 7 =   16

18 – 7 =   17

15 – 2 =   18

How do you make gold soup?

14	61	72	23	33	28
$+\ 5$	$+\ 6$	$+\ 6$	$+\ 5$	$+\ 2$	$+\ 1$
(D)	(E)	(N)	(A)	(C)	(U)

51	31	41	61	92
$+\ 8$	$+\ 7$	$+\ 8$	$+\ 7$	$+\ 5$
(R)	(F)	(T)	(O)	(S)

$$\overline{28}\quad \overline{19}\quad \overline{19}$$

$$\overline{38}\quad \overline{68}\quad \overline{29}\quad \overline{59}\quad \overline{49}\quad \overline{67}\quad \overline{67}\quad \overline{78}$$

"

$$\overline{35}\quad \overline{28}\quad \overline{59}\quad \overline{59}\quad \overline{68}\quad \overline{49}\quad \overline{97}$$

!"

Add the first two numbers. Write the sum in the box. Add the sum to the next number. Continue to add to solve each problem.

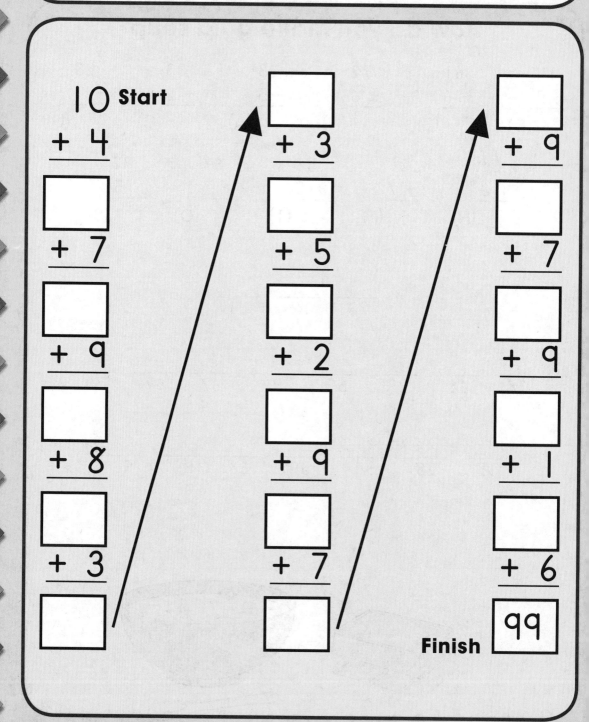

10 **Start**
+ 4

+ 7

+ 9

+ 8

+ 3

+ 3

+ 5

+ 2

+ 9

+ 7

+ 9

+ 7

+ 9

+ 1

+ 6

99 **Finish**

 CD-104366

Solve each problem. Cut out each puzzle piece.
Paste it on the space that contains the correct sum.

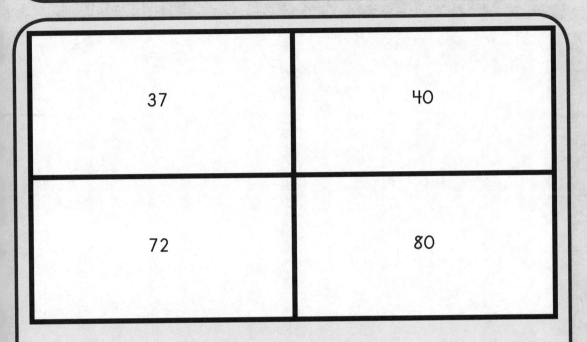

37	40
72	80

cut ✂

64
+ 8

28
+ 9

73
+ 7

35
+ 5

CD-104366

Solve each problem. Then, follow the answers in the maze to help the snail find the mushrooms.

14 − 5	33 − 8	41 − 9	16 − 8	55 − 6	88 − 9
55 − 7	81 − 5	53 − 8	19 − 0	77 − 8	52 − 5
51 − 5	67 − 9	81 − 2	29 − 9	43 − 8	22 − 4

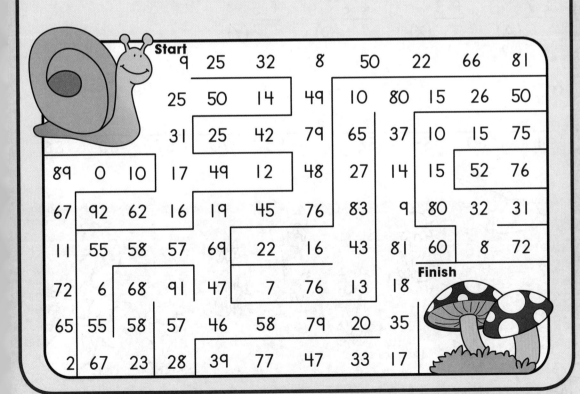

What do rabbits use to keep their fur in place?

16
+ 7
(B)

41
+ 9
(L)

58
+ 3
(H)

28
+ 5
(M)

53
+ 7
(A)

76
+ 8
(R)

55
+ 3
(E)

84
+ 1
(S)

31
+ 8
(Q)

65
+ 5
(P)

50
+ 7
(R)

41
+ 3
(N)

56
+ 7
(A)

37
+ 3
(X)

25
+ 6
(O)

81
+ 5
(Y)

" ___ ___ ___ ___   ___ ___ ___ ___ ___ "
61 60 84 58   85 70 57 63 86

CD-104366

Solve each problem. Use the key to color the picture.
36 = yellow   **47** = orange   **65** = brown   **76** = green

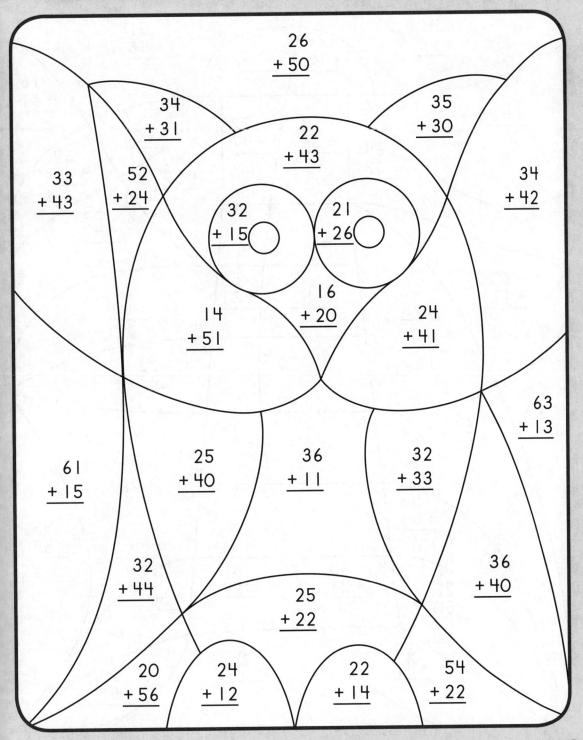

26
+ 50

34
+ 31

22
+ 43

35
+ 30

33
+ 43

52
+ 24

32
+ 15

21
+ 26

34
+ 42

16
+ 20

14
+ 51

24
+ 41

63
+ 13

61
+ 15

25
+ 40

36
+ 11

32
+ 33

32
+ 44

36
+ 40

25
+ 22

20
+ 56

24
+ 12

22
+ 14

54
+ 22

CD-104366

43

Solve each problem. Use the key to color the picture.
69 = yellow   75 = brown   84 = red   97 = blue

$$41 + 56$$

$$71 + 13$$

$$50 + 34$$

$$51 + 46$$

$$72 + 25$$

$$16 + 81$$

$$34 + 35$$

$$22 + 47$$

$$66 + 31$$

$$64 + 33$$

$$40 + 57$$

$$32 + 65$$

$$55 + 42$$

$$80 + 17$$

$$22 + 75$$

$$42 + 42$$

$$53 + 31$$

$$37 + 60$$

$$44 + 53$$

$$34 + 63$$

$$26 + 71$$

$$24 + 60$$

$$52 + 32$$

$$71 + 26$$

$$43 + 54$$

$$45 + 52$$

$$25 + 50$$

$$63 + 21$$

$$40 + 44$$

$$45 + 30$$

$$34 + 41$$

$$61 + 14$$

$$23 + 52$$

Solve each problem. Cut out each puzzle piece. Paste it on the space that contains the correct difference.

32	77
21	14

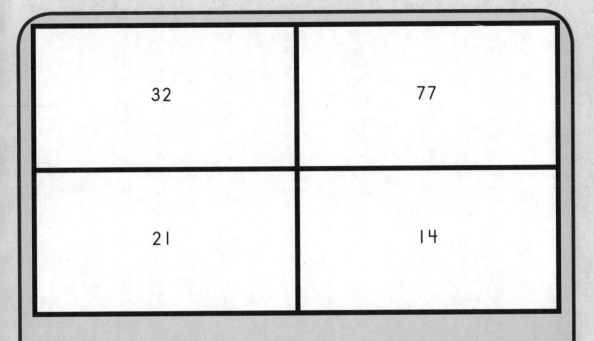

cut ✂

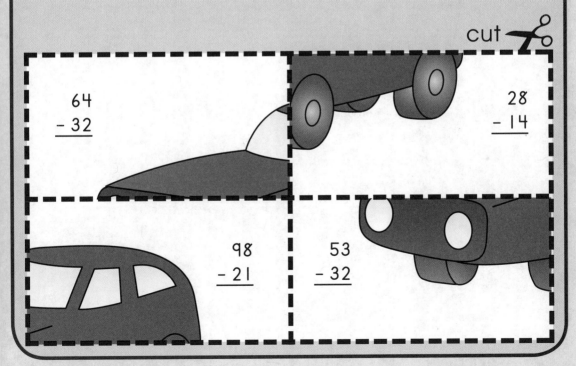

$$\begin{array}{r} 64 \\ -\ 32 \\ \hline \end{array}$$

$$\begin{array}{r} 28 \\ -\ 14 \\ \hline \end{array}$$

$$\begin{array}{r} 98 \\ -\ 21 \\ \hline \end{array}$$

$$\begin{array}{r} 53 \\ -\ 32 \\ \hline \end{array}$$

CD-104366

45

Solve each problem. Then, follow the answers in the maze to help the hen find her chick.

14 − 11	54 − 11	35 − 14	69 − 14	99 − 21	81 − 10

29 − 18	87 − 14	89 − 61	56 − 32	57 − 16	71 − 10

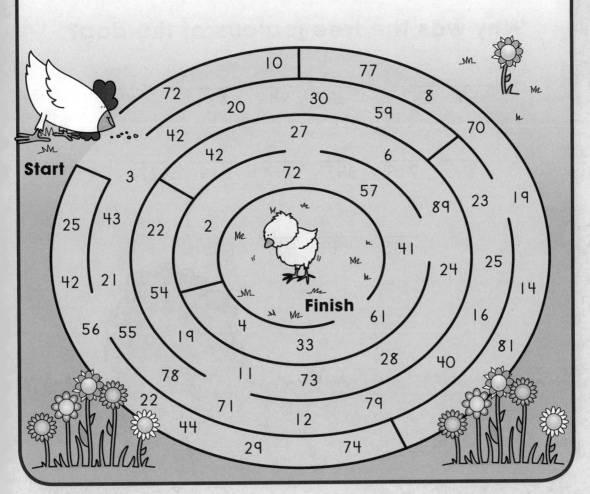

Start

Finish

Solve each problem. Match the sums to the numbers below. Write the correct letters on the lines.

302 + 5 (H)	556 + 3 (I)	440 + 9 (A)	142 + 3 (B)	425 + 2 (R)

823 + 1 (D)	343 + 4 (T)	212 + 7 (E)	601 + 2 (K)

Why was the tree jealous of the dog?

$\overline{559}$ $\overline{347}$ $\quad$ $\overline{307}$ $\overline{449}$ $\overline{824}$ $\quad$ $\overline{449}$

$\overline{145}$ $\overline{219}$ $\overline{347}$ $\overline{347}$ $\overline{219}$ $\overline{427}$

$\overline{145}$ $\overline{449}$ $\overline{427}$ $\overline{603}$ **!**

```
  498        658        809        428        863
-   5       -  4       -  8       -  7       -  2
 (T)        (I)        (M)        (U)        (L)

  779        523        217        594        327
-   1       -  3       -  5       -  0       -  6
 (O)        (P)        (N)        (Y)        (B)
```

What did the duck say when she bought lipstick?

___ ___ ___   ___ ___   ___ ___
520 421 493   654 493   778 212

___ ___   ___ ___   ___ ___ !
801 594   321 654   861 861

Solve each problem.

$$325 + 23$$

$$425 + 10$$

$$582 + 11$$

$$213 + 72$$

$$188 + 11$$

$$253 + 24$$

$$565 + 23$$

$$458 + 1$$

$$215 + 84$$

$$653 + 40$$

$$758 + 41$$

$$961 + 26$$

$$568 + 11$$

$$328 + 21$$

$$414 + 20$$

$$235 + 32$$

Solve each problem.

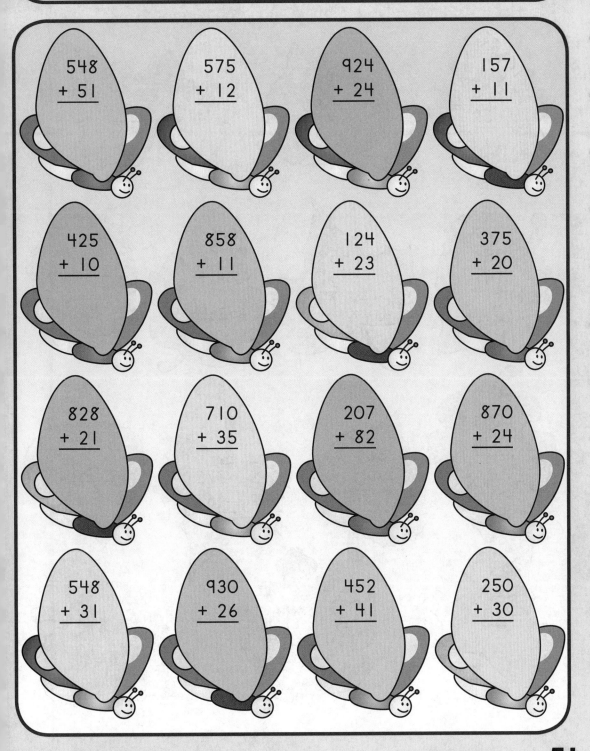

548
+ 51

575
+ 12

924
+ 24

157
+ 11

425
+ 10

858
+ 11

124
+ 23

375
+ 20

828
+ 21

710
+ 35

207
+ 82

870
+ 24

548
+ 31

930
+ 26

452
+ 41

250
+ 30

Solve each problem.

985
− 32

587
− 80

890
− 50

258
− 41

459
− 21

471
− 60

961
− 51

254
− 44

561
− 40

872
− 61

289
− 59

529
− 10

584
− 74

812
− 10

CD-104366

Solve each problem.

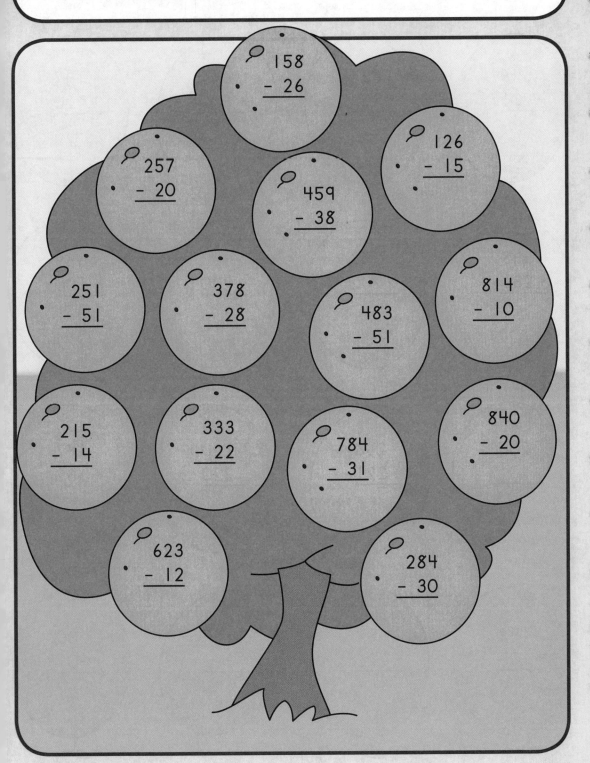

158
− 26

257
− 20

459
− 38

126
− 15

251
− 51

378
− 28

483
− 51

814
− 10

215
− 14

333
− 22

784
− 31

840
− 20

623
− 12

284
− 30

Solve each problem.

$$546 + 201$$

$$854 + 131$$

$$649 + 300$$

$$147 + 120$$

$$548 + 231$$

$$297 + 202$$

$$467 + 230$$

$$459 + 100$$

$$208 + 201$$

$$268 + 221$$

$$120 + 220$$

$$847 + 132$$

$$152 + 103$$

$$657 + 222$$

$$199 + 200$$

$$200 + 301$$

CD-104366

Solve each word problem.

1. Corinna saved 100 pennies. Quincey saved 110 pennies. How many total pennies did they save?

2. On Monday, the class picked up 151 pieces of litter. On Tuesday, they picked up 201 pieces of litter. How many total pieces of litter did the class pick up?

3. Jaden's family donated 120 items to charity. Sierra's family donated 102 items to charity. How many items did the two families donate in all?

4. Last month, the Lopez family recycled 129 items. This month, they recycled 450 items. How many items did the Lopez family recycle altogether?

Solve each problem.

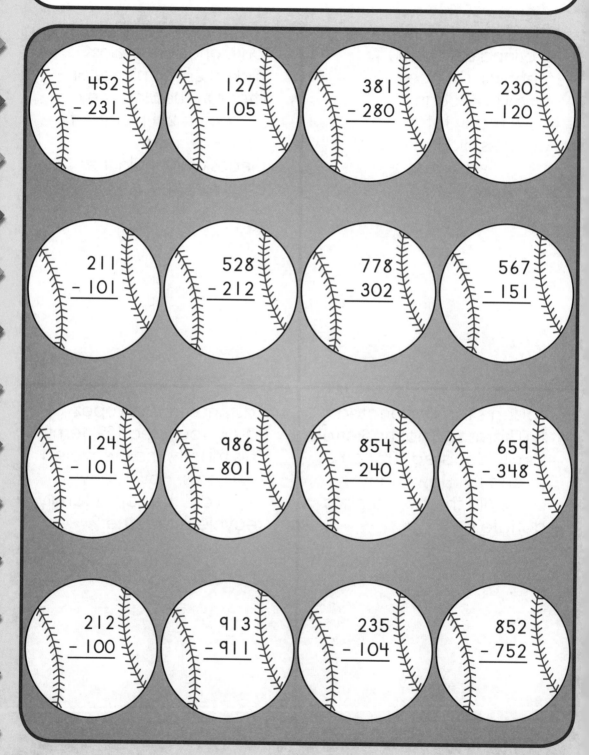

452 − 231	127 − 105	381 − 280	230 − 120
211 − 101	528 − 212	778 − 302	567 − 151
124 − 101	986 − 801	854 − 240	659 − 348
212 − 100	913 − 911	235 − 104	852 − 752

CD-104366

Solve each word problem.

1. Last year, Mrs. Avery picked 212 flowers and Mr. Emory picked 225 flowers. How many flowers did they pick altogether?

2. Last month, Rebecca and her dad bottled 350 large jars of honey and 250 small jars of honey. How many more large jars than small jars did they bottle?

3. The Chung family found 239 seashells at the beach. The Ramirez family found 212 seashells. How many more seashells did the Chung family find?

4. Amber collected 101 books. Drew collected 110 books. How many books did they collect altogether?

Solve each problem. Circle the three problems in each tic-tac-toe board that have the same answer.

A.

49 − 16	89 − 12	118 + 81
203 − 101	136 − 103	29 + 40
208 + 301	150 − 20	23 + 10

B.

15 − 14	159 − 158	11 − 10
159 − 101	100 + 1	456 − 301
325 + 21	20 + 41	28 + 41

C.

150 + 40	50 − 50	198 − 148
130 − 20	30 + 20	18 + 20
985 − 935	30 − 20	147 + 1

D.

99 − 14	19 − 13	140 − 120
88 − 12	10 + 10	170 − 60
950 − 930	421 + 50	98 − 10

CD-104366

Solve each problem. Cut out each puzzle piece. Paste it on the space that contains the correct answer.

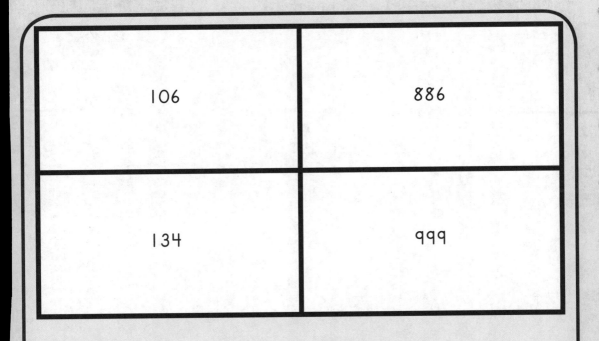

106	886
134	999

cut ✂

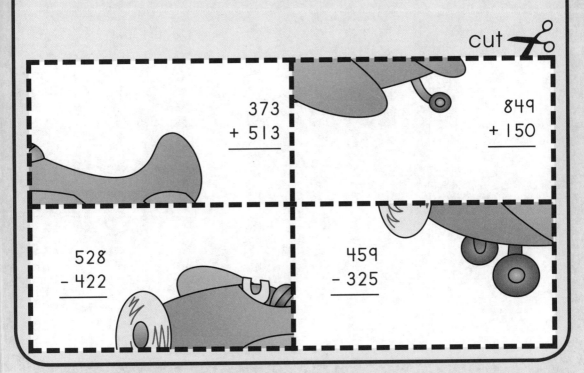

373 + 513	849 + 150
528 − 422	459 − 325

CD-104366